THIS CRAZY DEVOTION

Also by Philip Terman

Our Portion: New and Selected Poems
The Torah Garden
Rabbis of the Air
Book of the Unbroken Days
The House of Sages
My Dear Friend Kafka (poems translated into Arabic)

Chapbooks

The Four Seasons and *Like a Bird Entering a Window and Leaving Through Another Window* (with the painter James Stewart and bookbinder Susan Frakes)
Among the Scribes
Greatest Hits
What Survives

THIS
CRAZY
DEVOTION

Poems by

Philip Terman

Broadstone

Library of Congress Control Number 2020940113

ISBN 978-1-937968-70-0

Cover artwork by James Stewart,
used by permission.

Broadstone Books
An Imprint of
Broadstone Media LLC
418 Ann Street
Frankfort, KY 40601-1929
BroadstoneBooks.com

In crazy devotion for my family.
And for my friends, who know who they are.

I have perceiv'd that to be with those I like is enough,
To stop in company with the rest at evening is enough,
To be surrounded by beautiful, curious, breathing, laughing flesh is enough...

All things please the soul, but these please the soul well.

Whitman
"I Sing the Body Electric"

CONTENTS

Tormented Meshugenahs / 3

DREAMS OF POVERTY AND MIRACLES

Dear Li-Po— / 9
My Grandfather in Green / 11
Raven Slaughter and the Dream Machine / 13
I Wish I Remembered His Name/ 16
Reading Larry Levis' Last Poems / 18
All Her Life / 19
It's All Possible / 21
Darwish and Amichai in Heaven / 23
To My Friend in Aleppo / 24
Your Third Resurrection/ 26
A Minyan Plus One / 29
The Turning / 31

OF LONGING AND CHUTZPAH

1.   Mouth to Mouth / 35
2.   My Mother Cuts My Hair / 36
3.   My Mother's Other Life / 37
4.   My Mother's Poems / 39
5.   The Shopping Carts / 41
6.   All Our Years of Mother and Son / 42
7.   Pa / 44
8.   My Mother Died on Simchat Torah / 46
9.   The Exchange / 48
10.   Yahrzeit for My Mother / 49
        Coda: "put the put aside in the middle of the poem" / 51

THE DEVOTEES

The Sentinel / 55
They Sang Her a Name / 56
Koi-R-Us / 57
Kobe Bryant Competes with King David at the Gallerie dell Aceademia / 59
This Crazy Devotion / 61

My Father's Radio Interview / 62
One of the Immortals / 63
Zone Meeting with Mr. Goldberg / 65
The Service / 68
Bird at the Open Window/ 70
The Lady Slipper/ 72
Sweet Fruit of Recurrence / 73

GARDEN CHRONICLE

Garden Chronicle/ 81

After Later? / 101

Acknowledgments / 105

Tormented Meshuggenehs

Where are the crazy sages?

The ones who dervished across the hayfields
and paused to yawp a parable to the cows about the seven beggars,

that tale layered like an onion,
and when you peel it you wail like the child you still are,
wounded and wonderful?

And where are the rabbis who wandered
all over and off this world,
measuring distance between our dreams and the stars,

the ones who wrote the testaments,
the commentaries on the commentaries,
the interpreters, the ones who exclaimed:

You haven't seen nothing yet!
This world is but preparation!

Those meshuggenehs!

Summer harvest, we eat of the soil—
basil into pesto, tomatoes into sauce.

And our prayers: a little table talk, a lot of laughter—
and the children, inhaling their supper,
bodies bonkers with they-don't-know-what,

scampering across the field to the pond,
searching for koi, jelly fish, frogs, dizzy with this, elated with that.

In the next world, will we be greeted with white scarf and crown?
Will we be invited to share in the feast?
Will we speak the language that should have been our own?
Will we reach a companionable silence?

Oh, you so-called masters, disclose the secrets only you know,
what the worms are whispering beneath the earth you bow your bodies toward.
Enter our dreams and reveal the source of our yearnings.

We move from book to garden, from garden to book.

Now is the time to taste the fruit before it enters the fruit,
the way God consulted the book before creating the world.

Why look deeper than the garment of the moment?

We want to read both testaments, the laws and the love,
the patriarchs and the forgiveness, the silence that Buddha taught.
We want the dharma and the java, the rebirth and the vegetable love.
We're topsy-turvy for the duration,

for our daughters placing small apples into the dog's mouth.

See what I mean?
It's like water, isn't it?
It's like the dream we call our life.

DREAMS OF POVERTY AND MIRACLES

DEAR LI PO—

For my daughter, Miriam Xinxiu

I hope this finds you in good health,
as vigorous as you were when I last saw you—

Remember?

We were together in that odd place, mostly dark, and misty,
and there were peonies involved,
and you were sporting your bright red shirt with the gold buttons—

I never wondered who dressed you—

and you were reigning in that small red armchair I, too, sat in as a child,
the one I brought back from my parents' basement,
the leather seat a little torn.

It's true, when I first laid eyes on you,
in that obscure room, and you still had your baby fat,
you were holding a cookie in your hand and jabbering,
which unsettled me a little into an unfamiliar calm and, what with your round face,
I thought of the laughing Buddha or some kind of Dalai Lama.

Remember how, once, when we journeyed so far from that place,
and you sat on a towel on the sand,
you suddenly pointed at the empty blue sky
and I looked up into the enormous silence
and a bird appeared?

Li Po, wherever you are now, I want to know if you can still hear
the sky's music before anyone else.
I'm told that you are a crazy drinker, a real dabbler,
an extreme example, like your father, of irresponsibility.

Li Po, remember when you called me Gandhi?
I thought in respect,
but now I know in mockery of my stiff wisdom,
my serious sentimentality.

I hope you don't wander like your namesake
or like your father's people who travel aimlessly
with nothing to help them survive but words.

We built pyramids together.

Remember when I made you repeat letters after me
so we could speak the same language?
It was when I carried you in my back in the dark
        all the way to the water.

Li Po, shall we embrace the reflection of the full moon?

My Grandfather in Green

Chagall, you must have known my grandfather
who lived in the same province,
perhaps a few shtetls away,
and who pedaled fruit and scrap with his one-eyed horse

and so must have shouted out his wares on the dirt road
        of Vitebsk, your village,
and you must have, turning aside from the blank canvas
and looking out the window above the town,
heard his hawking Yiddish and noticed his pauper's cap
and rabbinical rhythms, then returned to your brushes and pallet

and began, this time with gusto, your *Jew in Green*.

You invited him to sit his weary over-coated slouched body down
on a couch of shadowed sacred texts, his face lowering,
as if in mourning, into his yellow beard,
his eyes distracted—such sadness you painted!—

He came, sat down, and at once fell asleep, you said,

exhausted as he must have been from hours floating
        above the town,
his enormous figure lifted beyond the snow-covered roofs
and blue-tiled churches and empty streets, leaning forward
        as if navigating the wind
with cane in hand and yellow sack slung back over a shoulder—

yes, that was him, Yussel, my grandfather you painted—
did you get his permission?—did you pay him his wage?—

the one, in the thumbed photo, dressed like a rabbi
with black cap and white garment shawled the length of his body
so he could, as it was written, touch the blue fringes
and remember God and the Commandments?

Did you put him on the canvas to get one more Jew out of harm's way?

Did you want my grandfather to represent the Holy One
          the whole village awaited,
a symbol for the drunkard for whom everyone poured
          a glass of wine,
the hunchback slouching through their dreams of poverty and miracles?

I want to know more about that green Jew,
and the Jew who inhales the snuff, who stares into an inward space,
his eyes fixed above the text laid open on the table, spread with yellow light.

I'd like to think that figure was Yussel, too, inhaling God,
his whole body sweetened by the habit—
and, especially, I want to know more about the Jew whose feet
          are above ground in an impossible leap
and whose head is turned around to stare into the eyes of the woman
          whose name means *beautiful*,
a vase of roses in her hand, her feet a few inches above the red carpet.

Because here it is mid-February, zero to the bone, the workday world about to begin,
the air turning grey, then greyer, then dark—

so mostly, I want to lie down beside the reclining Jew at dusk,
patches of light splashed through the grass, the spruce trees, horse, pig,
          house, lilac sky beyond,
thin arms crossed over soft blue smock, hatless,

musing on love, of course, and beauty—Yussel, Yussel—
did this insatiable artist paint you into the immortality you deserve?

Did he imagine you a dreaming poet, too?

Raven Slaughter and the Dream Machine

We could hear him a block away,
in the warehouse district, downtown,
corner of Chester and Euclid Avenue—

I had gathered my verses, finagled
my father's used Olds: "lock the doors,"
he commanded," and "roll up the windows"—

mid-70's, the riots still singed
in his memory, Cleveland a ghost town
from University Circle to the Terminal Tower—

a large patch of dark, a few stragglers,
a lead guitar screeching through
the dimly lit window, drums pummeling

like my pulse, seventeen and full of fear
and thrill descending into the depths
of what my parents drilled into me as

dangerous, but, fancying myself a lyricist,
not because it made more money than poetry
but, after failing at drums and guitar,

I knew the closest I'd come to girls
and fame would be whatever I could muster
in story and rhyme—after all,

I was the go-to-guy for sonnets
the jocks and freaks were assigned—
so I placed an ad in *The Scene Magazine*:

Lyricist looking for a band—
and the one call came, soft voice
whispering he had great chords

but what he needed was words.
Shaking—to the music or the jitters?—
I banged on the iron door, and he appeared:

long straight black hair, dressed in black,
six-inch Cuban heels, leading me into
the cavern, huge amp and three guitars,

and, slouched on the couch in the corner,
a rail-thin barely clad blonde
reading a book about Marilyn Monroe—

Let's see 'em, he demanded.
I handed him the lyrics: typed up,
alphabetically arranged in the blue folder

with titles like: "Brotherhood," "The Dream
Machine," "Religion Without God." Flaying
at his strings, he stuttered out

the first of my words, "Hit me once
before I go/I can't face the streets alone,"
then screeched to a stop

and stared straight at me,
as if in sudden illumination:
What the fuck does this mean, anyway?

It's a hit of pot, isn't it?
The manager says no drugs, no glitter.
What did I know? I must have sensed

that these rhymed confessions,
quickly scribbled in a teenage angst,
would get me nowhere.

But at that age, we'd do anything
that had any chance, even the slightest,
to take us away from school and into

the imagined fantasy we had to believe in
or go crazy. And so, when Raven asked
if he could hold onto them, that was enough,

more than enough when I saw, a month later,
an ad in *The Scene:* "Appearing at Euclid Tavern:
Raven Slaughter—and the Dream Machine."

I Wish I Remembered His Name

Before entering the classroom,
the warden sits me down in his office,
on his desk a photo album spread open:

guards and prisoners dripping blood,
--the famous New Mexico prison riot--
some lying dead in the yard:

To show you what can happen.
and make sure they're wearing
their regulation orange outfits——

as if I can do anything about
the truly scary one
hunched in his seat

in the center of the room,
mirror-sunglasses, all muscles, staring
at the floor, feet tapping

as if he would just as soon
be somewhere else,
his whole body in a fight position

as if, with so much as a glance
In his direction, he'll leap up
And tear your face off.

I don't know a thing.
I want to hear their stories:
Do any of you do any writing?

A thin tall bespectacled pale old man
in the corner slowly raises his hand:
I jot down every day, you know, stuff that I think about.

And another, young, too young to be here:
I write letters to my girlfriend, yes I do,
I write them but she won't write back.

Muscle man lifts his head
slowly, deliberately, towards
the front of the room,

speaking, each word
a boulder requiring
all of his concentration:

Yes. I write.
I write——
poetry.

ON READING LARRY LEVIS' LAST POEMS

The way we keep reading this dead poet,
one deliberate word at a time, until we arrive

at the last period in the last work.

But we know there's more,
we nudge the lovers and friends for letters,

we ransack the drafts,
turn over the boxes for every scribble and scrawl,
each stained slip of school verse he saved,

we strip the floors of his study for crumbled and tossed-off scraps,
partially scorched, mostly illegible, cross-outs and inserts,
alternative phrases filling the margins—

after all, weren't twenty lines of Gilgamesh recently discovered,
revising our interpretations, casting the characters in a new light?

Dangerous, we learn early in life, falling all over ourselves for another,
though that lesson leaves us, and so loss is what we agree on,
fools that we are.

It must be that we love our hearts breaking,
and the way, like a puzzle, we attempt to piece them back together,
cracked and flawed and hoping

the blood will keep pumping
for the affections we can't live without.

ALL HER LIFE

You don't know me.

I'm a palliative care nurse.
Do you know what that means?
I work with patients who are dying.

And I received an odd request. You know
when some are dying they get a last wish?

Well this woman's last wish——
I hope you don't mind this strange call——
is——all her life she's written poetry.

And now, her cancer has spread,
and she always wanted to know——I hope
you don't mind——from someone——

I got your number from the university——

I asked about someone who could judge
what was good poetry——
and they gave me your number——

if her poetry is good.
If she would have been a real poet.

We'll be moving her into hospice soon.

Might you mind looking at a few——
just a few——poems and tell her
if you think she was good enough?

That she would have made a good poet?

This morning she showed me a picture
she drew—many years ago, she said—
of a child—perhaps it was her?—writing

in the center of a round table
before a bouquet of flowers —roses I think—

that was what she'd have wanted for the cover
if she ever was able to have
a book of her own.

A book of her own, I remember her saying.

And then her face flushed
a little, and her eyes looked away.

It's All Possible

for Riad Saleh Hussein

Like a sudden explosion or an attack of the heart,
your poems arrive from Aleppo, that broken country.

Deaf, mute, handsome, "Expansive," I'm told,
"like Whitman, with an affection for alcohol, and women— a poetry star."

Until you were tortured, imprisoned, the psychic scars penetrating deeper,
then dying—one source claims, of "negligence," and another: "induced by
        heartbreak."

Your friends found you alone in your apartment curled on your bed,
shivering, hallucinating, begging for a sip of water.

Riad, no one in my country has heard of you.
But here you are: beautiful in this charcoal drawing:

Hair black and thick like Lorca's, sculpted face, eyes dark,
serious and focused at some nearby disaster,

diving into your ocean of images: birds, bombs—
Poor Syria like a bone between the teeth of a dog; a knife in the hand of a surgeon.

Riad, in the original, your words travel from right to left,
from your Middle East to my Middle West.

Can this translation give you back the voice you heeded in your soul's privacy?
You wanted *to build a room for a thousand friends.*

No end of your wants—
A pocket full of bells; an earthquake of wisdom; clouds under your bed.

Riad, I try to hallucinate with you, to know those erupting rhythms.
But what do I—raised in another scripture,

our people enemies cursing each other even
onto the next generations—have to do with you?

That's what I would inquire, if we could sit in my small study,
sipping tea in the light turning to dark turning to dream

that says it's all possible.
Riad, you wanted to *plough the galaxy*;

To live for all the dead; to place a river in the prison.
When, eyes closed, you were smoking a cigarette, did your demons ascend?

Little amounts of surprises.
Which I write down now, after you.

DARWISH AND AMICHAI SHARE POEMS IN HEAVEN

So let's be an open hand,
one of them says, *offering our time*
to the Gods.

    The other responds:

Even a fist was an open palm
with five fingers.

    And it goes on
like this, year after year, age
after age, these two souls hovering,

    indistinguishable in the light,

reciting their spirit-selves one
after the other, no longer grieving

    their respective exiles,

the breath of their words
shaping the winds
across the deserts
of their homeland,

    which is the same homeland,

and now they recite together,

    each listening hard
to the other's language.

To a Friend in Aleppo

for Saleh Razzouk

Saleh, the spear-shaped tomato leaves reaching out
into the sunlight, the yellow primroses glistening at the far-side
of the garden, the oriole defying anti-immigrant laws
soaring back and forth between properties and your hunger—for what?—

all this and more of all this,
more of this late spring-into-summer morning

and I wish I could bring it all to you, where you are,
where the bombs explode the buildings
and hearts to needle-edged fragments,
where the absurd horrifies the air—

all this beauty, all this serenity, this life I happen—
who knows how or why— to be living,
this accident of birth and circumstance, this chaotic explosion
that sent me here and you there—

and did your god and did my god sit down
and negotiate the terms of this destiny?

Now, here, the oriole lights out of the sweetgum.
Now, there, what birds can you be hearing through the buzzing helicopters
and the whipping planes and the rubble and the screams and the screams
            and the screams?

Here wings flapping.
Here a soft breeze ruffles my hair.
A distant dove's five-note song of mourning.

I wanted to write another pastoral poem about the jewel's glistening precision
            of this moment,
the dew- laden grass, the light-blue sky, the shadows stretched across the garden.

And you had to arrive with your complaints
about how there's been no electricity for three weeks
and about the car bomb outside your flat
and about the fanatics taking over your university
and about how your brother's shoes were stolen.

And, this morning,
when if one sits calmly and listens hard
we can observe the precise hour when spring turns into summer—

here you are again,
writing to me in your broken English
about how you can't leave because your son is still missing.

And about the oriole that just returned to the sweetgum
I don't tell you.

Your Third Resurrection

Sometimes we're called back,
who knows why, toward a part

of our lives lived through
and mostly forgotten until a few words,

a name, returns us to a café,
a familiar thin body, coffee, poems

scattered across the tabletop.
Richard, I found you again

in a used bookstore in Charlottesville.
I scanned my eyes across every title

in the poetry section, and there you were:
at the end of the last shelf—

I could have missed you, your volume:
Where Rivers Come From, Poems by Richard Solly,

your snapshot on the back: less hair,
the same mischievous smile—

on the cover a photo of Taylor's Falls,
Minnesota, where you lived and wrote

about your double afterlife
because, you continually reminded me

and Mary and Mary and Rachel
and who knows how many others—

your more than friends—companions,
you didn't have to say, of your spirit—

that you were not once, but twice, declared,
and by, you insisted, no less

than an ordained priest—dead,
and so you'd insist that all that extra time together

was free of charge, a gift on top of a gift.
Where are you now, Richard?

Google. Obituary.
Underrated,

a fellow poet said of you:
He defied death and defied suffering.

Fellow Clevelanders, fellow poets—
what else did we need?

Just an open café and a booth in the back
and a clean table to scatter our scribbles on,

trading them, studying them like cards,
our *poet's crapgame*, you joked—

yours about your Crohns and your cancer
and your blessed daughter, Rose,

who you said you were staying alive for,
and who you no doubt refer to

in your poem, "The Body Approaches the Soul"
where you sing: "Don't panic. I'll carry you

on my shoulders/into a garden; everyone
we have loved will follow...."

And all our back and forth—
what was it all about?

If we're lucky, Richard—our lives.

A Minyan Plus One

was taken from us on the Shabbat,
the most joyous of the holidays,
the only holy day even God Himself

celebrates, the emulation of Eden,
the day of completion. Before
they could perform the service, before

they could take their seats and begin
the prayers, before the ark opened
and the Torah revealed,

before they could rise and sway
and chant their portion, the book
opened like wings in their steady hands,

though they know the blessings by heart.
I didn't know them, but I knew them
in the way we know those raised,

no matter where we originated,
in the same beliefs our ancestors
inherited all the way back into

those mysterious origins,
those stories of creation and exile,
of miracles and complicated kings,

of commandments and wisdoms—
"welcome the stranger"—
spread across the millennium.

We suffer the same persecutions,
celebrate the same triumphs, chant,
in the same order, the blessings,

hour after hour, holiday after holiday,
generation after generation,
Torah portion after Torah portion.

Before that week's Torah portion,
a minyan plus one was taken.
When they would have once again

heard the story of when Abraham,
our first Patriarch of Chutzpah,
approached and argued with the Lord:

"Will you sweep away the righteous
with the wicked?" And God answered:
"For the sake of ten, I will not destroy it."

And so, as on other days, on that day—
He did. He allowed the wicked
to sweep away the righteous.

*And when the LORD had finished
speaking with Abraham, He left.*
And took a minyan plus one.

And Abraham returned home.

*For the eleven victims of the Tree of Life
Synagogue shootings in Pittsburgh, PA
on October 27, 2018.*

The Turning

The jeweled apples, the wind-rustlings—
these spectaculars
asserting their authority over whatever heartache
was breaking us.

Time for the red-tailed hawk to float
towards the sharp red and yellow leaves,
leading us to conclusions:

summer held its own,
the inevitabilities
of longing, the children's laughter under
the loud stars.

Migrating birds, what wisdom?

Season us with your autumn,
its glorious summation,
its desire that is a desire of embers.

To think
of this beauty occurring without us,

like the last glimpse of the swallows
as they disappear
toward their next chronicler,

the days equipped for flight.

To consider this apple tree—

to know that devotion,
that mission to blossom
and therefore fruit and fall
and be part of the larger earth.

A peck of the last remnants
left too long on the porch,
monument to our abundance.

We haven't the heart to eat them,
reminders of the bounty our lives were,
as we waited beneath, shook the limbs
and scattered the children.

We are becoming our nothing,
save for shadows
the apple tree limbs shapes across this page,
our lives a preparation for permanence.

We're thinning out into the pure moment,
listening to the wind's voice:

Turn, it says.

Turn to the beauty
that will outlast your sorrow.

OF LONGING AND CHUTZPAH

OF LONGING AND CHUTZPAH

1. *Mouth to Mouth*

At the pool, the drowning man saved,
lying stock-still on the deck: suddenly,

my mother loosens my grip
and surges through the swarm

of dripping suits and leans over
his enormous body, tips his head to the side,

pinches his nostrils—her chest tenses
with air, she seals her mouth over his mouth

and, like God breathing into Adam,
releases all of her breath into this stranger,

and I am full of anger and longing,
and he gasps and spits, his eyes opening,

the crowd stepping back and gawking
at my mother, who is hovering, and he rises.

2. *My Mother Cuts My Hair*

To save money, my mother leads me
to the bathroom, sits me down
on the toilet, flashes the rusty scissors
in the dim light, *The Honeymooners*
audible from the next room. She snips
until I protest, then snips some more,
sculpting me into the straight-A student,
the boy that helps around the house,
the boy she wants to be a mensch
and marry a Jewish woman but
doesn't forget his mother, building
her a home for her declining years
and, when the time comes, lights
a candle and recites the kaddish
on her yahrzeit. Snip, snip, snip.

3. *My Mother's Other Life*

Before we would go out
to dinner or a movie,
after a long day of who-

knows what, cleaning,
certainly, straightening
the confusion

from four sloppy sons
and a husband who had
his own private headaches,

my mother would stop
in the middle of our rushing
around and hollering

about who gets to ride
in the front seat and say,
calmly, *just a second*,

sitting down on a black-cushioned,
straight-back chair placed
beside the door solely

for that purpose: to rest
briefly, to deeply breathe in
and out until her heart

slowed down and her face
calmed. No matter how much
in a hurry we were, through

the yelling of my father's voice
and my brothers' hastenings
and my own, the motor running.

Who knows what settled her?
Perhaps she returned
for that brief spell

to when she was a girl
alone on the gigantic porch
of the rented yellow duplex

on 153rd Street off Kinsman,
near the small shul, reading
Gone with the Wind

cover to cover, her mother
studying for her citizenship,
her father's horse and buggy

clopping down the cobbled
street with its cargo
of fruit and vegetables.

She was where we weren't,
her name her own, her other life.
Slowly she'd look up and slowly

she'd rise in the sudden
silence, ours, to face the world
and us once again.

4. *My Mother's Poems*

You look sexy tonight, my husband said.

My mother reads from the poem she wrote
about the night of my conception—
open mic night, Bridge Coffee House.

After my introduction,
she half-runs to the stage and stands
tiptoe up to the too-tall microphone

and proclaims:
my son said I could read three poems,
but I'm going to read five—

to thunderous applause.
Homespun as they were,
she'd recite her poems anywhere,

to anyone,
at weddings and bar mitzvahs—
she was the one who stood up

in the middle of the meal
and read her rhymed verses—
filled with wisdom and good humor—

and it was me she'd call
in the middle of the night
and read them and wonder where

can she get them published?—
tales of her father selling apples
behind his one-eyed horse

through the Depression streets
of Jewish Cleveland,
of her mother getting a ticket

not for driving too fast
but for driving too slow.
I'd watch her type all day

at that long desk in the den,
pages she'd gather neatly
into thick bundles, punch three holes

in their left margins and clasp them
inside a cardboard folder,
design a drawing for the cover,

seal the collection with a title
and store it in the bottom drawer
with the others—

I hear her voice now—
head lowered, eyes squeezed shut---
proclaim that poem

that embarrasses me back
to my beginnings, her loving become my life,
her sweet pleasure become our poetry.

5. *The Shopping Carts*

My mother collected them,
pushing her purchases—
ice cream and pretzels, chocolate—
the seven blocks from Giant Eagle to her garage.

She parked them one inside the other
the way they rest at the store as if,
like the good hostess she always was,
she wanted them to feel at home.

If the store manager knew,
he didn't call the police.
Like old horses they kept their place,
as if they enjoyed their new residence,

no longer having to be loaded up
and bullied around the aisles,
abandoned at the checkout line.
Until discovered by the son,

always on the lookout
for sugar packets stashed in Styrofoam containers,
vines twirled around the chandelier,
smell of mold and mildew and unwashed flesh—

the ever-watchful son,
who wheeled them back to the store
by a circuitous route
in the middle of the night.

6. *All Our Years of Mother and Son*

No matter how large the print,
my mother still can't read *Leaves of Grass*,

though there it is, beneath her pillow,
in the Alzheimer's Unit, where she sits on the purple blanket
eyes transfixed on the floor: suddenly,

snapping out of whatever solution eluded her,
she stares me full in the face, parts her mouth,
shapes her lips into a semblance of a word,
struggling—what I understand
from all our years of mother and son—

the way her skin flushes with desire,
her eyes widen with wanting—
the child hidden just beneath the adult surface—craving,
as she often did, for beauty over truth—

to assert her determination to escape, pleading,

by all we have between us,
that I must grant this request:

to take her shivering hand in my hand
and lead her back to that world
she brought me into—

all this, and then darkness,
a slight shadow crossing her eyes,
glazed over, knowing somehow—who knows how?—
that she lost again,

now flaying her arms, a wounded bird,
flaying them up and down,
her chest rising, falling,
that alive thing rampant inside her flesh's cage,
that person she was,

that person of longing and chutzpah.

7. *Pa*

The grandfather my mother
called *Pa* I never knew,
though here's a picture of him
holding me on the front porch
of his rented duplex, looking
down at my infant body with
his immigrant eyes, singing
in his Yiddish tongue songs
he must have learned
in the shtetl that was Poland,
then Russia, then Poland again,
resting before returning
to his scrap cart hooked up
to his one-eyed horse or was it
rather when he sold fruit,
weighing it on the scale
that now hangs from the same
worn rope and rusty chains
in our kitchen, still cradling
apples and oranges and bananas?
Did he measure what he earned
to assure my future?
Is he whispering into my ear
that I won't have much
to remember him by
but I should grow up
to be a *mensch* and take care
of his daughter, my mother?
Nathon: forgive my poor attempt
to transform your dust
into these inadequate
words. All I have is this

curled and creased photo,
your suspenders loose
over wrinkled shirt,
your peasant's cap tipped
to one side, your mouth
grimacing at my attempt
to capture anything at all
of who you are and what
you might leave me with—
except, in the nursing home,
my mother mistook me
for you, and called me *Pa*.

8. *My Mother Died on Simchat Torah*

The completion of the annual cycle,
when we read the last portion,
when we begin to believe, as we have throughout the centuries,

that this time we will get it right and be finished with this labor,
this rolling up the heavy stone of the commandments,
like Sisyphus and his rock, and wrestling with —what to call it?—

It doesn't even have a name—that Holiness, that Tyrant,
one moment embracing us as if we were His children
and another smiting us as if we were better off as the nothing we were
before He claimed credit for creating us—yes,

this time we'll chant the last passage once and for all,
the one about Moses, the favored son, who He loved above all the others,
the one who He asked to do Him a favor—

to corral all of us complainers into that dreamland,
that grand retirement home, only to be told, at the last moment,
that, though he did wonders, Moses can see the place,
but he may not enter, all his yearning almost fulfilled.

"Better to have stayed a shepherd," Moses must have thought.
But we read: *No prophet has risen like Moses, whom the Lord knew face to face.*

Just as we pronounce the closing words,
for the how-many-millionth-time?—
clasping again to the hope that we're finished with all this repetition,

and just as the rabbi is about to seal the magnum opus for good,
and she raises her arms in benediction above us,
exhausted as we are from the long week of work and heartaches—
and we rise and sway and she squints,
assessing all the secrets that lay hidden there,

and just as she is confirmed in her decision to roll back the scroll
and once again place the pointer under the opening words and chant:
In the beginning, God created the heaven and earth—

at that precise moment, between the last words and the first,
between the standing up and the sitting down
      and the starting all over again,
just as the Sabbath sun burns down into its deepest flame—

you decide it's time to depart.
You don't need to recite all those words again.

You know the whole story by heart.

9. *The Exchange*

Mother, I allowed you to live alone in your decline.
I agreed to place you in what was not your home,
nursed by others who did not love you
so that I could live my life without the burden you bore for me
when I, too, was helpless.
When I, too, could not dress myself, you dressed me.
When I, too, could not feed myself, you fed me.
When I, too, could not clean up after myself, you washed me.
When I, too, could not walk by myself, you held me up.
When I, too, screamed, you sang me to sleep.
And so we exchanged our lives for our lives
and what you did for me I should have done for you.
And now, alone in my house, as you were alone in your house,
Calling for you, as you called for me, and sometimes I would answer.

10. *Yahrzeit for My Mother*

Seven years you've been gone.

Today—the Shabbos, Yom Kippur,
the holiest of our holiest days,
a day you would have cherished,

I'm sitting here, before the service,
sinning: sipping coffee, sneaking down
these words which, according
to Leviticus, is work. But

it's no sweat to resurrect you
on this holiest of holy days,
you, without whom this

would be just another day
in a series of days
that make up a life.

When I was ten, under
the great domed ceiling,
I stood up when you stood up
and sat down when you sat down

and something in my youth
turned to you and said:
I don't believe this.

You went on singing.

And I turned back to the page
with its strange symbols
the hours from then until now
are still teaching me to comprehend.

Seven years, mother, a lucky number,
on this holiest of holiest days, even luckier,
and on the *Shabbos*, no less—

Fix your tie, you say. *It's time
to go to shul. Stop sinning.*

Coda: *put the book aside in the middle of the poem*

the one that speaks of laurels
moist grass

let your bed remain
unmade the blankets
tossed about as
during love

your face as it is

leave your clothes loose
around your body
however wrinkled

and slide
into those chinese slippers
that move like leaves
across the carpet

don't bother turning
a light on
or locking your door

simply allow it to creak
in the recent wind
and steal yourself
down the road
that leads out of town

past the dim lights
yellowing empty spaces
behind storefront windows
the last stop sign
the abandoned temple

until all that remains
are pinpricks of light
filtering through the black
yarmulke of sky

look into these   look into these
until you discover
again those words
of the blessing you spoke
each night before bed

for the small breath
of your mother's lips
against your cheek

THE DEVOTEES

THE SENTINEL

for my daughter, Bella

As the mythical yellow bus
slows down on Scrubgrass Road

in the early dark and December frost
to gather in once more our child

and haul her off into the world
that for each of us is a separate mystery,

the very last image she will glimpse,
as she turns around one more time

before rushing up the steps and
hurrying towards the one seat

in the back to bury herself
into her own private music,

is your body under the porch light,
coffee cup warming your hand, how you waited

like a sentinel every school-day dawn,
dutiful until the very last moment

of her departure and, in some fleeting
moments in her adulthood, in the midst

of some confusion or loss or triumph,
your attention is what she will remember.

THEY SANG HER A NAME

Mourning doves and robins
and the school bus
slowing down and pausing
and picking up our child

who once was so distant
we wouldn't know how
to imagine her.

Remember traveling across the world
to gather her in our embrace
and claim her as our own?

Where are those who birthed her,
without whom she would be as unfamiliar to us
as everything else we will never love?

Do those who made her
call her in a language
this chosen one still hears in her sleep?

They sang her a name, then,
because of forces beyond comprehension,
set her down in a public place and hurried away,
heavier in their absence.

And we appeared.
And lifted her up.

And sang her another.

Koi-R-Us

How much of your life
would you devote
to swimming
like a koi

in the heart-shaped pond,
corner of the hay field,
late summer goldenrod,
the heron for now absent?

How much attention
are you willing to pay
to flash orange,
bright as the sun level

with the horizon?
Yes, some are caught
and sold—a small business
for your daughters—

five bucks each,
ten for a butterfly
—*such a deal!*
Customers would arrive

from far south as Pittsburgh,
north as Titusville,
whole families camping out
on a Sunday afternoon

with their rods and lunches:
Koi-R-Us, you'd joke,
sighing: *koi vey!*
at the intrusion. But

the kids copped cash
for college and ice cream
and a short course
on capitalism.

How much of your life
would you devote to floating
through your daughters'
dreams,

diving down deep
where the water darkens,
rising into the light,
for the bread?

KOBE BRYANT COMPETES WITH KING DAVID
AT THE GALLERIE DELL ACCEDEMIA

The crowd circles the masterpiece,
around and around, wondering
how something this beautiful

can be possible, this perfectly shaped
human that so astounds us we wish
to protect it from the vibrations

of our own footsteps— suddenly,
all eyes shift and stare
at this other familiar figure

of famous flesh and blood,
wearing purple Lakers' shorts
and shaking hands with tourists,

a modern hero stealing our attention
from the one we've waited in line
to view, all morning and into the afternoon,

the shepherd boy who inquired
of the king about that uncircumsized
nine-foot bronze-helmeted Philistine:

Who does he think he is? he spat out:
To defy the ranks of the living God?
So he gathered his stick and smooth stones

and became a stone himself, defending
the civil liberties of Florence, his eyes
permanently fixed, the way Kobe

measured the angle and distance
of the swish, daring the opponent.
I was—weren't you?—Kobe, scoring

all those points on my parents' back-
of-the-house b-ball court, shooting
my famous jumpers and foul shots

all day at the splintered backboard
and netless rusty rim until dusk
blurred into dark and the ball

shattered one of the garage windows
and my father yelled that was enough
for the day. Meanwhile the hero

maintains his steady posture,
the position preserved, we hope,
long as the spirit lasts.

THIS CRAZY DEVOTION

"Back soon. Went to pick up some 'friends,'" the note said, scrawled in pen, taped to the side door. I had rushed over after my shift at Burger King, still wearing my orange-and-yellow-ketchup-and-mustard-stained shirt and paper-sailor's-cap, "the fastest and sloppiest burger maker in the history of the franchise," my manager joked, as I placed the frozen patties on the electric conveyor grill, constructing them the customer's way to the rhythm of pick-any-one-of-his-songs, this crazy–though it wouldn't be "cool" to admit it—devotion—I was among the converted since my older brother slapped *Greatest Hits Volume I* on the turntable and headphones around my cranium and song after song baptized my soul—what was it?—something other than what school and after-school Hebrew-school couldn't shake, that this Jew, like me, with the imperfect voice, like my own, with words that sounded suspiciously like words I would write if I could, that this existence—unlike the other options— my father tired after a day at the used car lot, my brothers' science hieroglyphics, college an insurmountable cliff—all I had were all these "poems" I was writing since I could write—was possible. And this older friend, this Joel, claims, to our skepticism, he knows him from the early days of the Village, this hero at once distant as fame and close as my own voice, was in town, and I should come and meet him, his "friend"—and so I waited, outside the side door with the scrawled note, in disbelief, and fear, for something to happen—I didn't know what, until, finally, Joel's Impala pulls into the driveway, and Joel gets out, and a woman with thick black hair gets out—wearing a white mink stole and a cross, and Joel turns to her and says: "Sara," and turns to me and says "Phil," and so—I knew from the pictures—the wife, but where is he?— and we proceed into the basement, and Joel puts on some music—the Doors?—and there she is, in an office chair, swirling from side to side, reading a *Playboy*— I'd read she was a model—tall, beautiful, mysterious—were her eyes sad? Did she have a mercury mouth? Was her voice like chimes? She didn't speak much. Across the dimly lit distance, she passed the bowl to me and I, floating in my burger king uniform toward a life impossible to imagine, passed it back to her, chanting *your saint-like face and your ghost-like soul*—until Joel looked at his watch: "Should we call him?" And she, looking up from her *Playboy*: "No. Let's not wake him up."

for Howard Simon

MY FATHER'S RADIO INTERVIEW

If it could have been scheduled,
he would have discussed the theories
he'd developed of selling used cars.

It's an instinct, he would have said
to the schlemiel host of the local NPR station.
It's a lot like gin rummy——never speculate.

*Sometimes you're dealt a good hand
but more often it's a foot.* Elaborating,
he'd quote Shakespeare:

*To be or not to be. That is really the question.
Con- sumption be done about it?*
[pretending to cough into his sweater]: *of cuff! of cuff!*

He would have rejected the theories
of who was born in Grant's tomb and vote
for Mo Hair, not Dan Druff.

Imagine: six foot four, he'd rise,
light a cigar, blow a smoke ring, pause,
and reveal his golden nugget:

Don't smoke. It stunts your growth.
Leaving the studio, he'd pause,
turn around and assert: *look at me.*

I could have been seven feet tall.

ONE OF THE IMMORTALS

Beyond the reach of death, those rare spirits,
so long alive and hearty they build ponds and trap
and plant every spring hundreds of trees
to make certain the land will renew beyond them,
whose bodies seem ageless, as if they somehow discovered
the fountain of youth in their secret souls, who rise
early and quickly eat and quickly get into their truck
and set off to check their traps and clear brush and mow,
barely breaking for lunch, so devoted are they to their task,
impervious to distraction—forget the dark—until their labor
is done and their rest is deep. Such a man was Shryl,
one of the ageless ones, one of those you'd shake
your head at and say, "he'll live forever," and he does,
like each of God's patriarchs, leaving his heart-earned legacy,
committed to maintaining his family and his property
onto the next generation—trapper and planter, father
of children and grandchildren and great grandchildren—
countless, and therefore blessed, as the stars.

After he left what else
could we do but follow him

to the pond where we gathered
cattails and Joe-Pye, pursue

his spirit into the woods
for ferns and white pine?

Two turkeys distracted us
and we hoped we'd discover

a few of their dropped feathers
so we could collect them, too,

for the bouquets we'd arrange
in the burleys he'd wear all day,

trudging through the swamps
to check his traps and discover

arrowheads or planting hundreds
of spruce. Just on the verge of dusk,

the woods suddenly quiet,
we traced him into the deeper silence,

where we knew we'd find him.

for the Hood Family

Zoom Meeting for Mr. Goldberg

Early morning, the only two up,
me writing on the couch, Artie
coming down the stairs and looking
for his keys: *I'm off to get some bagels*,
and I want to come along,
he insisting I needn't—
stay in, it's cold, you're writing,
why should you schlep?

I contending I wanted to,
and it continued like this,
two old Jewish *knockers*—
but he was twenty years older—

this tug of war we do—
I want to go, no, stay, I'll be right back,
like those ancient men
at the corner table
at Corky and Lenny's Delicatessen,

kvetching all morning into the afternoon
because *kibitzing* is the way
they choose to spend
their remaining time on this earth.

And Artie was one of those—
he loved to lie on the couch
and watch his beloved Yankees
and, after Susan asked him to,
would refuse to remove his shoes
why should I?

And so we drove to Balthazar,
that Synagogue of Bakeries,
and he parked in front

of a no-parking sign—
and when I pointed it out:

let them arrest me!
If they've got nothing better to do!

And when we arrived back
at the house they were all up
 and hungry and Artie, laughing:
We did it! We got the bagels!

Who were we to each other,
Artie? is what I'd ask him—
I'm the schlemiel, he might say,
who dated your sister-in-law
after your brother died—
ten years already—

and there was such a warmth—
the word in Yiddish: *heymish*
"comfortable, familiar, cozy"—
in his presence I forgot
he wasn't another brother—

yes! he said again: *We did it!*
Phil and I! We got the bagels!

On the ventilator for two weeks,
the call from Susan:
they're taking him off—

and a small window for each of us,
including Artie, on his hospital bed,
masked like an alien,
the rabbi reciting the blessing:

the confession before departing,
bringing atonement:

It should be recited with a clear mind.
Artie, did you have a clear mind?

If a person cannot speak,
it may be said in their heart.
Artie, you said it in your heart.

It can be recited by both men and women.
Artie, you were a mensch.

On any day, even on the Shabbat.
It wasn't on any day. It was a Thursday.

If a person's children are present—
your children were present—
You should exhort them to follow the Torah.
Artie, you exhorted them to follow your Torah.

One should not leave you alone.
We said, in our broken words, our farewells.

Did you hear us?

And, at the last moment,
all of us in our little windows,
including you, Artie—we sang
The Lord is our God, the Lord is One.

And we thanked the doctor and nurses. Each of us.

for Susan Terman

THE SERVICE

And with a man you shall not lie as with a woman....

Despite the passages in Leviticus
which cause him consternation
he doesn't know what to do with,
Ben embraces the tradition—

wearing not only the yarmulke
but the knotted fringes dangling
from his shirt: he touches them,
as it is written, to remember

the mitzvahs and do them,
and so always in the grocery store
or the laundromat he's noticed
and commented on, his body

a Torah passage surrounded
by interpretations of his fellow citizens,
the tradition he turned to
and learned the language so thoroughly

he can read from the scripture
and teach Talmud to the Christians.
Once, after a holiday celebration,
a stranger appeared, unwashed,

black beard unkempt, eyes glassy,
stumbling, stammering.
We backed way. Ben approached,
offered him cake and lemonade:

How do we know he's not Elijah?
For the diminishing congregation
he mows in summer, shovels in winter,
cleans the sanctuary and the bathrooms,

the recreation hall and the rabbi's office,
interprets the week's portion for the monthly newsletter,
corrects the cantor when she misses a trope.
Are the doors secure? The pews dusted?

Is the ladder needed to change the eternal light?—
this appointed one assuring the shul
is kosher and the worship can commence
according to the commandments:

What a blessing!
Serving the House of Hashem....!
If it only weren't for Leviticus 18 and 20, he adds—
to himself, his silent petition, his abomination.

BIRD AT THE OPEN WINDOW

Beginning with her garden,
the garden her life was,
beginning with how she was time eternity embraced,

the way she was embraced by the sari her Swami
bestowed upon her that she wore twice,
once for her beauty—tall and thin, a heron in her shyness,
the way she'd arrive and depart silently—
and once after she passed to grace her spirit's magnificence—

enlightened as she was, selfless as she was, humorous as she was,
flower-gatherer, friend-gatherer,
how her passions were fruits always in season,
fully ripe, catholic in their sweep and scope,
Taoist in their meditative calm, quietly Zorbatic,
old-fashioned in her Forties dresses and her dignity,
in her consideration—

take a seat, have some wine, enough about me tell me about you,

wise in the ways of drawing you out
the way she knew how to draw out
the purple-tongued petals of her irises
and the multi-musical soul of her beloved child
on whom she bestowed all of her accumulated dedication—

yes, she wore satin and antique dresses,
yes—she wore theatrical hats and berets,
yes, there was some Italian mama in her,
and she could do a Jewish shtick,
and she could belt out a torch ballad at 2 AM
and direct a musical so flawlessly
she would disappear into her own creation—

and was there a flowering season without blossoms in her house?
And was there an occasion when she didn't request a poem?
And was there a rhythm to which she didn't boogie?

And that last summer—she burned down into her essential fire,
her refusal, her gentle but insistent rage, such bravery, such nobility—

the way she steadied herself in her solitary struggle,
the way she never bowed or broke--how heroic,
this helper of so many hearts, still, toward the end,
continuing to heal us, even as we tried to heal her—

insisting on more music, and wine
and harvesting whatever vegetables her hands nurtured
and ripened and picked and washed and sliced and arranged—
what meal did she prepare in that house wasn't a feast
for the fortunate ones who called her *neighbor?*
and she, who served us all—

we earth-tenders, inventors and weavers of garments and words,
builders of local-lumbered palaces that last beyond our lifetimes,
protestors against the preposterous wars,
advocates of alternative resources, we stargazers, we moon howlers—

alone in her house, which she made our house,
bird at the open window—

The Lady Slipper

Illegal to pick in Minnesota,
discouraged anywhere without permission,
hidden in ferns, mossy hummocks,
imperiled right here in Pennsylvania—
so difficult to propagate
even Darwin couldn't cultivate it.

As only a gardener would know another gardener,
you knew that she—whose attention is so acute,
can spot, even in the darkest, dampest woods,
almost any flower—has never, on the lookout
as she always is, come upon one, shy as they are,
preferring dappled to full sunlight,
shadowed leaf mulch, hidden, they hope, from deer,
sensitive—who isn't?—to hydraulic disturbances.

For her, they were in the stratosphere,
right up there on her wish-to-see-before-she-dies list
with that almost impossible-to-find mysterious mushroom, the morel.

Once, when a local forager who-shall-remain-nameless
led her way beyond his cabin into the woods
to his secret patch and allowed her
a long longing morel look, he—we hope—joked:
Well, now we'll have to kill you.

But you, who also shall remain nameless,
risked your neighborly reputation
and uprooted one, the Queen's—no less than Aphrodite's—Slipper.

You snuck it in the back of your truck with a bucket of aerated soil
and presented it to her, your fellow nurturer
of the rare, the terrestrial, for what requires patience
and attention and a lot of luck—
this little lady, hidden, modest, vulnerable, pink.

for The Maestro

SWEET FRUIT OF RECURRENCE

Where are we at the moment of arrival?
Are we where longing rests?

Does desire meet its demand?
I am on top of you, or,

the world spinning as it does,
you are on top of me.

Can we call it luck, the way
this moment was reached,

all the fortuitous failures and close calls?
Or is it a kind of fate,

the way the past seems inevitable,
how all we've said and done has led to this?

The love of the long married—
kids in school, mid-afternoon.

We ate gefilte fish with extra hot white horseradish
and apple chutney, a strange craving she had.

It wasn't a ritual and we weren't commemorating
anything tribal other than our hunger

and opportunity's small window—
that brief interval, more intense

in its restrictions,
seasoned, spiced flame, bite and burn:

horseradish on gefilte fish.

Do you mind if I watch you dress?

Why have I messed with books all these years?
Why have I tried to find assurances in words or stars

or, worse, dreams I never asked for?
What made me think listening to the rain

or walking into the dusk
would somehow change me into something better?

And all this time it was really those moments
when you rose and dressed that counted,

and now, in the dawn silence,
the first birds sing out of the rain to assure us

another day will unfold for our pleasure.

The Allegheny took my wedding ring,
slipped it off my finger

one mid-summer afternoon as I sprawled
in the kayak, arms extended,

hands flapping the surface,
my wife and daughter drifting off—

no hurry,
letting the season have its way with us—

we searched, between rocks,
eyes squinting for something sparkling

in the sunlight but we knew by then
it was either buried beneath the mud bottom

or its yellow-white-rose gold
was on its merry way to Pittsburgh

bearing its abstract and primitive inscriptions
that originally compelled us,

that beastly hot day on overcrowded Canal Street,
to purchase one for each of us

to wear as long as we'd last—longer,
like this river,

that doesn't begin somewhere
and end somewhere else.

We walked around the cemetery at dusk.
We didn't have any big issues to discuss.

Our children were at the kitchen table
doing homework.

Late summer, apples scattering beneath their tree,
crickets orchestrating the air.

When we returned, our children
were still at their homework.

You went back to canning beans.
I resumed my place in this poem.

Can you hear the changing?
The children upstairs, stirring,

hurrying, dressing, brushing
for the rooms and bells,

for the long hallways,
the imagined glances. I want

to shout to them: *Yes!*
We're still here, your mother and I!

This house of your childhood!
This life you will barely recall!

Now they are rushing out,
breakfast and backpacks,

door opening,
door closing.

Neglectful I am, not preparing for our loss.
We wake and the children off to school

and it's work or the garden
and those few errands that provide the rhythm

of our days—and those occasions, like now,
when I remove myself from our lives

so that I can meditate on our lives
and frame something beautiful,

these moments composed out of some obscure need—
we don't search that deeply, we don't wish

to waste our heartbeats on some indefinable thing
even the major prophets had a difficult time

articulating, though we read them before sleep.

Months ago you rolled the thin pancakes around
the cottage cheese and froze them for this December

morning, as the sun glistens the ice crusted branches
and snow weighs down the spruce needles. Now,

you heat them on the cookstove and I wake, the way
my grandfather woke, to the smell of dough frying in butter.

We smother them with sauce from strawberries
we picked and sliced and mashed with sugar and stored

last summer or was it the summer before last? I'm confused:
how time slips—sour cream sticks in the hairs of my beard.

Or is it my grandfather's tongue that savors each crumb?
Slender hours rolled like crepe around our preserved souls,

sweet fruit of recurrence, these Ukrainian delicacies—
each taste swallows me back to him, that peasant rabbi.

You examine your garden the way I study this page.
How many blossomings.

Alright, it took a life of grief
and joy to reach this place,

such as the gestures
our fingertips describe around the scars,

recalling us again our mortality,
these bodies made of flesh and fire,

even when we forget ourselves,
even in that upstairs bedroom on 12th Street,

and the sweet silence afterward.

GARDEN CHRONICLE

I *will meet you at the origin point of every garden.*
—Sohrab Sepehri

Garden Chronicle

Early spring is no time for Torah,
not with the deep purple and white irises
shouting at us, not with the bleeding hearts—

I'm talking about this world, there is no other,

not now, not with this climax of spring
and newly discovered peonies
in the shade garden between the house and the barn.

A dove takes on extra mourning at evening
a shadow-bird it embraces against the sky,
that place we all meet, but

how do you say farewell to a spring dusk?

I'm not suggesting we own this hour,
the disappearing light, the soaring birds,
I'm not in any way implying no one else
can have it too, just as it is, now, here,

I'm not greedily requesting each night be balmy
as this one—we know the dust-mote of our existence—

we know our names as the pink streak of the light's
disappearance—but, really, how many do we have left?

Spring dusks, I mean.

With a bagful of books
and a vase of peacock feathers

I walk to the pond of many peepers—
morning's endeavor,

two frightened ducks
and nine stubborn geese,

morning with its sky and bells,
its hollow tree,

its frogs floating on the surface,
singing like Isaiah urging repentance

from the Chinese willow.
The beebalm at the water's edge

is the chosen people longing
for the swallow to swoop

and skim across the surface.
Queen Ann's lace attend a sermon

the wind is winding down
and the dragonflies are resurrections

of my ancestors—
herring dealers and Talmudic scholars.

Can we measure up to what
has been bestowed upon us?

It's not, after all, Moses and his ultimatum.
It's just a certain helplessness before all this beauty.

The book we prostrate ourselves before

requires more than eighty cows
whose manure the Henrys are spreading

in rows across their field along Mill Road,
the nutrients mixed with the March snow—

good for the soil, good for the corn they'll plant
so the cows can produce more come next year.

And if these kosher cud-chewers knew
their flesh will be sliced and separated
from the bone, soaked in lye, stretched
over a wooden frame, scraped
and measured into a page onto which
the scribe will script sacred words?

Oh! These cattle who feed
on fodder and sleep in straw and moo
all day long in the mud—

dreaming they will be so clean
no one's hands are pure enough to touch them,
even with the tips of our oily fingers,

dream that we will hoist them above
our shoulders and display them
around the congregation, dream
that we will kiss their hide
with our chapped and dusty lips!

April Fool's Day and Charlie's back to deliver the oak,
seasoned with maple and cherry—
fifty dollars a load.

He parks his beater at the barn's edge,
hobbles onto the bed and tosses the logs
he'd split 18 inches to fit our stove into the dark

back of the barn, the way, hours ago, we tossed hay
onto the potatoes—dank wet world for them to root
down in, down, down, into the wonder-hole,

where we are half the time.
Evening, still a little cool but promising cherry blossoms,
more than a child can count.

Now I stack the wood for winter,
one season folded inside another the way time's ingredients—
past, present and future— are mixed and swirled
like yeast and flour and eggs
with your wooden spoon.

Daffodils and hellebores and tulips, purple and yellow,
the profusion of the periwinkles--and so we listened for your call,
for surely, after how lofty we've elevated you over the years,
slicing the fruit and placing it on our good china beside
the homegrown homemade grape jelly we labored over
just for you: jam *royal*, we labeled it, because it half-rhymes
with your name— and so when the first geese squawked
and screeched onto the pond, and the robins, two of them,
romanced from lawn to apple tree branch, and the red-headed woodpecker
resumed his chiseling task on the oak, and the red-winged blackbird
and the wren and the mourning doves gathered in their crazy congregation
around the holy ark of the feeder—we craved—turning over
the compost and edging the shade garden and planning
the raised beds and planting the seeds--for your clear whistle
and now, early, May Day, coffee and the chorus—*where?*—
there— look up!—flautist in the sweetgum, chest out, orioling your orange.

Local Amish sawmill—
odd and end slabs and throwaways
churning through the long pipe
spitting out pieces of bark
onto a small mountain of mulch,

which my wife—never the spendthrift,
dickering with the owner
for boards to build her raised beds—notices:

"10 bucks a truckload," Jake Byler says,
all business, stern-faced, straw-hat tipped back.

"And if the load goes over the top of the bed, an extra 5.
And don't forget to bring your shovels."

The whole family at work building
the raised bed, following the plan—
in the southern corner of the garden,
fastening together the cedar boards,
wheelbarrowing the mushroom compost
from where it was dumped, smoothing
with the shovel the surface soft,
so soft a small stem can erupt through,
poking tiny hole after tiny hole the size
of a mole's escape, tightly placing
and packing in one seed at a time, our breath
its blessing, then the next, and the next,
securing each plant to rise from its dark
earth like some messiah we can believe in.

The garden strengthens hands—

the corn up and out, roses overgrowing the arbor,
the strawberries for now safe from the squirrels—

why look any deeper than the garment of the moment?

My perch is a woodpile, an open window
of fresh cut hay and wildflowers,
nothing to do but pay attention,

to listen to the hunger song
of those three tiny wrens straining
their beaks deep inside the straw-filled opening
of the green bird house
we purchased at the Amish auction
and secured to the apple tree.

Nothing left to do but allow
the shadow to sweep over us.

Don't tell me Isaiah was completely clearheaded
when he told us to turn our swords into plowshares.

Don't tell me Moses spent weeks drafting his mountain song.
That robin isn't studying any lexicon.

How long can we follow the movements of that oriole
as it traces its hunger from apple blossom to apple blossom?

White-pink petals drizzling,
fields spread with mustard seed and colt's foot,
and the robin floating across the garden *dizzies the silliness out of me.*

So I borrow from Whitman,
but I need a ballast at a time like this,
or else we'd float off into a soft air I *wish I could sing of*,

and that phrase is James Wright's,
the wind brushing the fallen apple blossoms across
the shadow of the tree they floated from.

So what else to do with all this time
than sit under these blossoms
and try to blossom myself?

In this spring tease—
we open windows,
break out lawn furniture,
scrub the grill,
rototill and weedwack
and mow and plant
and check out
the purple tulips
and pink peonies
and the tiny robin
in the nest on the rafter,
its mother scurrying off
to snatch the green blueberries—
time to store down coats
and heavy sweaters back
to the back closet—but—
this is Northwest Pennsylvania,
where Winter the Trickster tricks us again—
air cooling, temperature dropping:
wind, then rain, hard, fast—
isn't that sleet?—

then flakes, fat—
if this were December
we'd call them pretty,
we'd sit and stare out the window
beside the woodstove,
retrieve our Russian novels
for the long haul of hibernation—
but now we worry
the flowers freezing,
the blossoming trees fruitless—
and so, at dusk,
as the wind dies down,
we cover up what we can
with anything available—
turned-over buckets
and trashcans,
tarp the blueberry bushes
with soft blankets,
preserving our labor
against what we can't control—
one eye on the hope,
one eye on the forecasts.

Dickinson rows in Eden,
we hoe in the garden—

twilight, straw hats
brimmed with sweat.

We clear the corn of weeds—
the crabgrass, timothy,

purslane, sorrel, chickweed—
these undesirables we pull

out of the rocky soil, clenching
our hands into fists, tugging them

out by their roots, tossing them
into the yellow bucket, down

the rows, soundtrack of crickets
and robins, leaves brushing our skin,

music of steel against hard dirt
and stone as the traffic dies down

and the cricket-song emerges
out of the star-lit field.

Rows of peppers, rows of garlic,
rows of onions, rows of weeds, too,

but rows of tomatoes, rows
like lines in stanzas, and so

the garden is a poem, its verse
a little formal, a little free,

studied closely by the hummingbird
analyzing the bee balm, one red flower

at a time, skimmed over by the dove
flighting from hay bale to nest,

critiqued by the chipmunk nibbling
the strawberries, revised by the finch

uninhibited in the blueberry bush.
They only want what we want.

❁

Wouldn't we prefer to work outside among the bluebirds?

Early June, late evening,
as they build their nest inside their customized box
on the arbor of the climbing roses?

Companionable creatures,
the way these two journey together,
weaving their house,
avoiding the sparrows?

But these endure, roosting their beauty,
tracing each other from apple tree to arbor to apple tree.

Now, in the gray light after an all-afternoon rain,
one taps on the window,
interrupting our serious attention to frivolous details,

a better model of behavior than Leviticus—

we want to hear them, so much music beyond our reach,
we wish to go out among the stars and become no one again,
          as we once were,
before all this aching, and now the bluebirds sing

over me and our daughter who,
in her last hours of childhood,
charges across the just-cut field to climb a hay bale,
solitary against the horizon—she sits, listening, dreaming:

remember when we had no idea who we were?
We still don't.

What is this thing, this body, still unformed,

what is this pulling inside us, this beating we count, lying awake,
this pulsing we hear, but still don't believe, that will stop any time it wants,
without warning, this deepest part of us that decides when it has had
    enough of us?

All afternoon and into the evening we dream that way.
But what would we do, afterward,
if a day suddenly opened up, every hour of it, dawn to dusk?

It's ours, and all our longings, will we finally sort them out?
This one from that one, unspooling all those knotted strings?

And what would the sages say about a midsummer evening?
    That it's detrimental to ambition?

The bass notes of the frogs croak that I'm doing something right doing
    nothing much, recording the moment as it happens:

the enormous bee reading over my shoulder wondering if I can compose
    a poem that would frame this little eternity for a thousand years.

And who can sleep with the moon so full and yellow, rising now,
    close enough to eat,

like the earliest apple of the season, the trees full of them: yellow transparent,
    from the old country—

did my grandmother's tongue taste them, too, when she sewed the nightgown
    and lace scarf my mother inherited?—

Famous for drying, freezing, sauces and wine, but not good for storing,
    so reach up, pick and bite—gold coins in the sunset—warm in
        your palms,

sweet juicy swallows, and I want to write lines beautifully realized as this moment,
which doesn't plead or declare its inadequacies,

but only shakes its lush-leaved limbs and ripples its pond's surface
across the season into whatever happens next.

the old wheelbarrow is junk now
yet it hauled   cornstalks   potatoes   tomato stakes   straw

once it was filled with weeds
once it bore its burden of leaves   horse manure   seedlings before the plantings

carrier of split wood   from barn to side porch
of stones   from woods to garden's edge
of harvest vegetables   from soil to table

carriage for princesses   dressed in sequins and gowns

steadfast   silent in the weeds
rusting in its own dignity

content to be contrasted to the more famous poem
and then a bent wheel   a broken axle
on which nothing depends

Almost evening, you lead
your old friend around the garden,
pausing at each raised bed,

the black Buddhist robes
covering up his US Army
service number tattooed

along his muscular arm.
Back then, he did it all:
the divorce, the heroin,

the anger, the abandoned
son. When he called for help,
they put him on hold

longer than he could stand
and he broke
the phone in half.

Never without a gun.
And then Nam.
How many did I kill?

12-Step-everything,
the meditation.
He started walking. Viet Nam

to Auschwitz.
I took the first step,
and I knew. I knew.

Strolling in the soft light,
a bald-headed bird hovering above
the lettuce, the onions,

the garlic, the tomatoes,
the potatoes. *All this growth!*
Such abundance.

I've forgotten how I arrived here,
on this garden bench, observing
the robin flighting into the apple tree,
this mid-morning in one of my few allotted summers,
considering the dust I will become and, yes,

I've lost the thread of my existence
and the reasons and the elaborate purpose
I carefully constructed, not having prepared

for the limbs of this spruce tree spreading
its shadowed branches into some abstract design,

never counting on this soft breeze or factoring in
the raspberries' full redness to distraction.

And the more I sit among the flowers—
the roses and the irises and the peonies—
the more like a flower I become.

And once you've passed through the door of poetry,
you can never die in the same way again.

Where were we between the creation and the revelation?
At the table with four freshly picked tomatoes.

we picked all the grapes
we could reach
one here one there,
in bunches

some clusters   up top
down below

we filled our pecks
with tomatoes   peppers
onions

stored squash
in our basement

filled our ears with birdsong
our eyes with late blossoms
our faces with warm rain

our flesh with breasts and lips,
behind an ear   around a thigh

The garden says: *change.*
It continues: *become spectacular.*
   Obey the wind's command,
then turn into something else.

And the garden concludes:
   time to speak of emptiness,
to forget yourselves,
   to give up what you're not—

   lumbering bodies, idiotic worries—
and know you are built for flight,
   that even the basil left long after
the season is not lonely,

nor the morning glories nor the last
   hollyhock left beside the house—

time to save moments aside from eternity,
    some afternoon like this one,

    that we can return to, like the book
left open in which we read:
    every hour is the anniversary of our death,
the pages turning in the wind's hands—

whoever we were then, however
    we managed to survive it, that brief
arrival and departure, it will take
    the rest of our lives to uncover,

    our achievement, each thought
bringing us closer into our flaming
    hearts. Will we be together
in the emptiness? Will we spill

into each other's ears the abundance
    of our affection? Wind uplifts grasses,
September's sharp sun softening.
    We want to see the whole thing,

    the burning flames, the dispersed ashes.
We want to know where it all goes,
    the garden enacting its dying
in preparation for its next life.

We wait for the school bus
and our happiness as those leaves
sail fragile to earth, ready
to begin their changes.

We're ready, too—

the light afternoon rain,
the crickets and the cooling breezes,
the tomatoes' flush and the harvest,

then the end of the first day of school
when these seven suns appeared
out of the mist and the geese honked
their farewells.

We want to be like those xenias
holding onto their rigid and spikey beauties
long after the lilies have fallen away.

We've gathered everything
into the center of the garden to burn.

And the raspberries—
we've picked all we could
for their last transformations.

We've drained the machines,
gathered wood, spread the beds
with flannel sheets, down comforters,

embraced the holy books
and danced around the synagogue,
each of us called forth to appear beneath the canopy
to chant the last words, then the first,
reciting our recurrence, like these leaves.

And now the school bus and our happiness
have arrived.

AFTER LATER?

asks our child, wanting something,
whatever that is, beyond "in a little while,"
or "sometime soon," the unforeseeable future,

no set time, farther than the horizon,
on top of the sky, around the bend,
outside this moment we're in,

as if "later" is an hour
that you can point to on a clock,
or a date on a calendar.

How will we know when we arrive
at "after later"? Perhaps we're there,
according to whatever someone told us

"before earlier," whenever that was—
all those things they said would happen
must surely have occurred, as in

"when you're older," according
to some mysterious measurement
my daughter seems to grasp

about that time beyond time—
when it will take place, she believes—
whatever it was I promised her.

Acknowledgments

The Bridge Literary Journal:

"Married to the Allegheny" (included in "Sweet Fruit of Recurrence")

CCAR Journal

"With a bagful of books"
"Early spring is no time for Torah"
"Don't tell me Isaiah was completely clear headed"
"And what would the sages say"
(included in "Garden Chronicle")

The Cortland Review:

"Mouth to Mouth"
"My Mother Cuts My Hair"

The Fourth River:

"Willie Wheeler"
"Sweet Fruit of Recurrence" (as "How Many Blossomings")

The GoodWorks Review:

"My Mother's Poems"
"The Shopping Carts"
"All Our Years of Mother and Son"
"The Exchange"
"put the book aside in the middle of the poem"

Image:

"My Grandfather in Green"

Jewish Currents:

"Pa"
"Tormented Meshugenehs"

Jewish Journal:

"Again, These Blintzes" (included in "Sweet Fruit of Recurrence")

Lake Effect:

"Reading Larry Levis' Last Poems"

The Laurel Review:

"Kobe Bryant Competes with King David at the Gallerie dell Accedamia"

Nine Mile Arts and Literary Magazine: "Koi-R-Us"
                                        "The Lady Slipper"

One Magazine: "It's All Possible"

The Pittsburgh Post-Gazette: "Darwish and Amichai in Heaven"
                                        "The Sentinel"
                                        "A Minyan Plus One"

Poetry: "My Mother's Other Life"

Sheila-Na-Gig: "Dear Li-Po"

Tar River Poetry: "Raven Slaughter and the Dream Machine"

Terrain.com: "To My Friend in Aleppo"
                                        "Bluebirds" (included in "Garden Chronicle")

Tikkun: "My Mother Died on Simchas Torah"

Vox Populi: "All Her Life"
                                        "Such Abundance" (included in "Garden
                                        Chronicle")

The Working Poet: "The Turning"

Several sections included in "Garden Chronicle" appeared in *The Four Seasons*, a handsewn chapbook in collaboration with the painter James Stewart and the bookbinder Susan Frakes. Sections of that poem also served as the text for a song cycle, composed by Brent Register and published by Metropolis Music Publishers: Alry Productions.

"A Minyan Plus One" was translated into Hebrew by Hagit Grossman and appeared in the Israeli journal, *Iton 77*.

"My Grandfather in Green" was translated into Arabic and appeared in the Australian journal, *Al-Iraqia*.

"My Mother's Other Life" appeared in my collection, *Book of the Unbroken Days* (MAMMOTH books, 2005).

Many thanks to the artist James Stewart for permission to reproduce the drawing on the cover of this book. For more information and other examples of his artwork, please visit his website, stewartpainter.com.

About the Author

Philip Terman is the author of five full-length and four chapbook collections of poems, including, most recently, *Our Portion: New and Selected Poems* (Autumn House Press) and *Like a Bird Entering a Window and Leaving Through Another Window*, a hand-sewn collaboration with the artist James Stewart and bookbinder Susan Frakes. His poems and essays have appeared in numerous journals and anthologies, including *Poetry Magazine, The Kenyon Review, The Georgia Review, The Sun Magazine, Poetry International, Extraordinary Rendition: American Writers on Palestine*, and *99 Poems for the 99 Percent*. A selection of his poems, *My Dear Friend Kafka*, has been translated into Arabic by the Syrian writer and translator Saleh Razzouk and published by Ninwa Press in Damascus, Syria. He is a professor of English at Clarion University, where he directs the Spoken Art Reading Series. He is a co-founder of the Chautauqua Writer's Festival and coordinator of The Bridge Literary and Arts Center in Franklin, Pennsylvania. Terman's poems provided the text for three song cycles composed by Dr. Brent Register and, on occasion, he performs his poetry with the jazz band, Mark DeWalt and The Barkeyville Triangle. More information can be found at www.philipterman.com.

Designed for Broadstone Books
by Larry W. Moore,
set in Perpetua.
Printed by
Bookmobile.